ONE MORE CIVIL GESTURE

Poetry Pamphlets by C. E. J. Simons

Progress Bar (wordwolf press, 2010)
No Distinguishing Features (wordwolf press, 2011)

ONE MORE CIVIL GESTURE

C. E. J. Simons

ISOBAR
PRESS

First published in 2015 by

Isobar Press
14 Isokon Flats, Lawn Road,
London NW3 2XD, United Kingdom
&
Sakura 2-21-23-202, Setagaya-ku,
Tokyo 156-0053, Japan

http://isobarpress.com

ISBN 978-4-907359-08-9

ACKNOWLEDGEMENTS
Poems in this volume have previously appeared in *A Tower Miscellany, Magma, Oxford Poetry, Poetry Matters, The Liberal, The Reader, The Times Literary Supplement*, and prize publications for *The Cardiff International Poetry Competition, The Martin Starkie Poetry Prize*, and *The Wigtown Poetry Competition*.

COVER IMAGES
Sandro Botticelli, *Pallade e il Centauro* (detail), Uffizi Gallery, Florence, courtesy of the Italian Ministry of Cultural Heritage and Activities, and Tourism.
Author photo by Tina Burrett.

for Tina

For wonder is the child of rarity; and if a thing be rare, though in kind it be no way extraordinary, yet it is wondered at. While on the other hand things which really call for wonder... if we have them by us in common use, are but slightly noticed.... Now the singularities of art deserve to be noticed no less than those of nature.... And as among the singularities of nature I placed the sun, the moon, the magnet, and the like – things in fact most familiar, but in nature almost unique; so also must we do with the singularities of art.

(Francis Bacon, *The New Organon*, Book II, section xxxi)

Chomei at Toyama, his blank-
et hemp, his character a rank
not-to-be-trusted river mist,
events in Kyoto all grist
to the mill of a harsh irony,
since we are seen by what we see;
Thoreau like ice among the trees;
and Spenser, 'farre from enemyes'...

Derek Mahon, 'Beyond Howth Head'

CONTENTS

ONE MORE CIVIL GESTURE

TATAMI

You'll go far my son, she said among the cows –
alfalfa in my hand and the smell of dung.

Not *One day all this will be yours* –
they weren't our cows. What was mine was

an acre of buckwheat by a river-berm,
the smell of hay bales after a storm.

Twenty years on, and still it's clung.
Far gone is right. Hush-slide of a paper door.

Out of Shinjuku's hamstrung hearts
I slip into my own home like a thief.

Manitoba from ten thousand miles away
has miniaturized to a blind room:

a dozen interlocked *tatami* mats
have brooded through a twelve-hour summer day

and breathed out acres of grassland
from the grass that they'd once been –

this golden fleece was mown when it was green.
Like mine. My mother taught civility and art

and a medicine I couldn't understand.
Once more a child in the dark, I reach for her hand –

before the room airs, a lungful of open field:
the gift box of meadow-grass

unribbons its treasure-seals
and all for a time's alfalfa and manure.

But before I can let the old pasture go to seed
the night-breeze stirs

and Manitoba follows my mother's ghost
down the apartment stairs.

I loosen my tie as if eye to eye with a bull
and one more civil gesture could cost me my life.

THE SPEAKING CLOCK

Most ring up during business hours –
but some call through the night's white noise
and these I comfort and decoy,
as the artificial heart

of a wound clock under cotton gauze
calms orphaned animals.
Once you took your mother's hands
and asked her many questions.

Later at uncivilized
hours of penitence you'd call
for unconditional love disguised
as cliché or parable.

She's gone. Now things are going fast.
I can lead you by the wrist,
adjusting what you gain and lose
and whose mistake is whose.

Between the pips, before the third
tone there is time for 'you and I' –
time for all your half-sprung words
and pliable alibis –

but I'm not nearly so precise
as the pendulum you counted on –
your mother's opposite advice
at dusk and dawn.

UNI

comes from the sea
as far from *Kythereia*
as this Hokkaido market-stall –

as far from Knossos
as my father's wood-axe,
my backwater bull,

my jokes about prairie oysters –
as far from Aphrodite
as the diet

of runway model and run-away.
In the *nishoku-don*
it nestles down

on a bed of blood-red roe:
bloodflecked gold doubloons
spilt from a purse of veins –

the all-knowing salmon's
unborn suffering –
roe slick as the clear pearls worn

by the goddess, when she comes
pierced by sea-droplets
at earlobes and navel,

nipple-glisters blow-
dried by the Zephyr,
flesh paled, blonde-locked

by Botticelli's
family-friendly spell,
curves rolled flat

as damp dough –
anodyne to the aphrodisiac
of the peep-show.

Before you lift the stippled prize,
the golden yolk,
the bifurcated mound

from her bed of black thorns,
before you warm her raw quiver
with hungry breath, pray:

to Cytherean Venus,
to Aphrodite,
more than love-goddess,

the goddess of *ika* and *uni* –
as her mosaics
at Crete and Paphos show.

To taste it is to know
the flesh of gods –
sublime profanity –

to forget the prairies,
my jokes about prairie oysters,
my father's wood-axe,

my backwater bull –
and for a moment shiver
and shrink, like old Uranus

at the chill
of Saturn's slate-black sickle
against his balls.

If you know your Fleming, you may remember the scene
(the best bits never make it to the silver screen)

in which, just before the visit to Crab Key
James Bond drinks a bottle of Canadian Club whiskey.

He takes it into the garden of Beau Desert
and watches the sunset's last efforts

fail, and feels the 'Undertaker's Wind'
breathing out from the centre of the island,

cueing the tiny gold bells of the tree-frogs
in the palms. Bond pours slug after golden slug,

and keeps adding ice in the dusk – and drinks, and drinks,
wondering why he's drinking. Then the 'blink-a-blinks'

(as Quarrel calls the fireflies), start their sexual morse
in the darkness around him – a wanton randomness.

Soon he'll scull across thirty miles of oil-black sea
to glimpse his *Venus elegans*, his Botticelli's

Venus from behind.
At which point the shadow that crosses his mind –

and the mind of the boy with the tattered paperback
going to pieces by torchlight under his Mackinac

blanket and bedsheets – will darken to a scar.
The Bond of the knitted tie and the dry martini,

the Bond of the high-nine card, the Aston Martin,
the old Beretta and the new PPK

was a world away from Pembina and Fort Garry,
as far as any man from his numbered sobriquet,

far from the boy who had never tasted alcohol
and could only dream of girls diving for cone shells,

a boy years away from the Morse code of actual sex –
sex's underground facility, with its megalomaniac's

five-star dining, its lagoon with a giant squid.
Twenty years later and I'm no more intrepid.

But for a moment – a page – the English spy
with the six-shooter and the glass of Canadian rye

came close enough to Manitoba's fields and farms
to let the prairie boy think that in his twenties

these mental escapes might be more than fantasies
if he could only learn to perform, armed and unarmed.

Now my mind goes back to that pause before the kill
like a crab-boat nosing home against the dock-piles,

and though I'm still a cowboy compared to Bond,
with my own fatal showdown not yet at hand,

I've no need now for the gun or the golden whiskey,
for the burning drop from Walkerville, or Gimli –

no need for the dreams of honey-traps and spies,
of *femmes fatales* with caviar-dark eyes,

dreams of jungle airfields, palm trees and fireflies,
or a shell-diving girl from an island paradise,

her dripping white bikini complete with diving knife –
the dream of a blonde who can take care of herself –

since in you, I found the last – and all the rest
drifts with the fantasy out of the past

each time I kiss you, each time you towel your hair
after the beach – or a bath – each time we prepare

for our next departure from the usual.
So here's to you, my Bond girl, my Honeychile –

impossible to mistake or misconstrue
after the dénouement, after the rescue boat's overdue

promises of other sunsets and other islands
lull us towards that Undertaker's Wind.

FLOTSAM
(twelve days after Cyclone Nargis, 2008)

He looked like a pensioner out and about
on a Sunday morning, enjoying the sun.
We were searching for wounded, idling the fanboat,
and called out to him to join the evacuation.

The Irrawady Delta was a jumble sale
in a flooded car park, where all you could buy
was corpses, unless you felt inclined to bail
and bilge-pump your way down to a rotting paddy.

He stood on a patch of earth four metres square.
On one half, he'd built himself a shelter
from palm-fronds and sheet plastic.
A few hundred metres behind him, the shipwreck

of his temple had run aground, its rooftop *zedi*
a snapped mast. He raised his robes like Eliza D.'s
petticoats to keep them dry. I eyed his inventory:
a five-kilo bag of rice – a bag of dried chillies –

a week's worth of grey stubble on a teak pate.
With a long stick, he stirred the flotsam, the way a barcarole
eases his gondola down a quiet canal –
except that he stood still, while the city-state

reeled around him. We watched him salvage detritus –
boards, bottles, tires – anything the cyclone
had spun loose from the Great Wheel. But when we tried
to dictate his survival – mosquito net, Malarone –

he told us the salvage wasn't scraps
for his hovel. No. He was trying to rebuild the temple.
I pointed to the floating corpses
and asked him if God had made an example

to prove a point. He seemed unconcerned:
'Some grains are for the wind and some for the quern –
we do not grieve for the flower or the thorn –
those who are gone have already been reborn.'

So I asked him if none of the dead were greedy
for more life, if none of them had fought –
'Some were ready,' he said, 'and some were not ready,
but they were all more ready than they thought.'

MARCELLUS

I'm the one who said, 'Something is rotten
in the state of Denmark.' – So even if
you don't know me, you know me – and what's to know –
second lieutenant – king of the graveyard shift

(thugs, drunks, and jarkmen stumbling to the muster
any time between midnight and six o'clock) –
single father – chin-grizzled at forty –
quick with the cutlass, the partisan, the matchlock –

veteran of the Polish campaign, paid off
but never pensioned – gentleman without portfolio –
passed over for promotion at every turn –
left standing in the Kronborg's backstage shadows.

After the ghosts, the murders and suicides,
I laid low while young Norway's ski patrols
hissed past the royal park-pines, the drowsy pickets,
and hushed the kingdom to a new control;

I kissed my boy and rode out through the rastel –
one man, one pony, and a well-stocked pung –
travelling by night until I'd crossed from Zealand,
an oath to a dead prince bitter on my tongue.

Now the job he bollocksed up, I do in style –
revenge for hire – no theatrics, no subplots –
assassin's work with poniard and hebenon,
cleaning the slate of regicides and despots –

work that pays well, though I'm a wanted man
for watering down the stock of tragedies.
I sleep in caves – lurk in dead ice landscapes –
hunted alike by the player companies,

strolling bards, prologues, poets, licensed fools:
all want me dead for emptying the chronicles
of bloodbaths that would make a good fifth act –
they want court mayhem, not the careful kill.

I will persist, and quietly disappoint
Northern European literature
till the spy novel and a colder war
prove that my hits can please the publishers –

until the velvet stage machinery
of silenced pistol and garrotte replace
the poisoned Bible, the madman's rant,
the sleeping groom with blood smeared on his face.

KUROGO

Our heroine, damasked in pancake makeup
weeps without tears into a lacquered teacup,

wafting her sobs across the narrow stage –
someone's been murdered, someone's been betrayed –

and, like a puppet, showing more life with less,
declining from her posture's rigid axis

she lists stage right, as if one string were snipped.
The wading crane on her kimono dips

its head into the blue silk, disappears
under the surface, a dropped fishing spear.

Her 'shadow' bends over her in a black hood,
leaning in to light her tragic moods

with the butt-end of a smoking tallow candle:
she the full moon, and he, invisible,

the sun. By convention, we agree not to see him –
like stage machinery, or a superfluous limb –

and as we train our eyes to the display,
to look straight through his mimic shadow-play,

so each of us may slowly learn to see
our shadows: the lost souls who accompany

our wounded movements and our broken paces
and in confusion and darkness light our faces,

our secret tears – for them, the forgotten them,
though we think we cry for the princess and the kingdom.

And so the hooded figure leaning in at my side,
reaching up to my face, is a student suicide:

tied to me forever, another victim of chance –
Cinna the poet, Cordelia, Rosencrantz –

a silent girl who walked the boards in the sun
and walks them still, but for my self-expression,

lighting the survivor's mind with guttering guilt,
a gestalt of the dead and unfulfilled;

she makes me imagine heckling the performance
calling, *Can't you see them? Don't they deserve a glance,*

or a speech of their own? Who'll write a speech for them?
But of course I don't – I sit back and agree to pretend

my shadow's just another absence of light
no different from the light that created it.

Past the footlights the tragedy's all but wrapped up –
the princess kills herself with two elegant cuts.

The shadows outlive the revengers and their cause,
but take no bows and suffer no applause –

and soon, upstage and down, they congregate
to help the fallen idols to their feet.

AS HE LIKES IT
(for Tina B.)

Kate seems a kitten when you're hot and fierce –
Helena's bait-and-switch, Rosalind's guile
pale in comparison to your long game.
You'd lift a ring from Portia while she riled
the dinner-guests with platitudes of justice –
you're wild as Beatrice dressed in her disdain –

but any other wife would be a shadow,
'the name and not the thing' – Hermione's,
Cordelia's, Desdemona's pieties
bore you, you claim – but your Petruchio
sees the deep lodestar, the love that terrifies –
Titania with the potion on her eyes –

and thanks his stars that he's a forest-beast –
safe, now that Oberon's antidote is lost.

HOMESTEAD

You say you're fine to be the other woman,
swear that out in the woods it's not really that cold –

you get what you want and don't care for cat's cradle –
but I've seen the woodcuts, the wolf shadowing the fold –

know that black-letter bargains are struck to be broken –
how one glimpse through the star-frosted leadlight, one glimpse

of hearth, cot, rocking chair, a blessing on the lintel,
her beech-brush sieving its yard of gold

tears the charm of your casual word from your neck –
how the chuckling fire draws your eye to the mantle

where no looking-glass throws your own misery back
but the length of a loaded musket glints.

MORAY

Murderous granny
long in the two
teeth that remain,
scalp blue-rinsed
to mottled green,
hides under the stairs
with a cloudy eye
upturned to the shallows'
mirror-sky,
tripping and tucking
her victims away
to soften and sweeten
to tinned pâté.
All pretence strips
off with the old lace:
a narrow skull,
a vacant face,
eyebrows plucked out,
ears lopped off,
emphysema's silent
water-cough,
jaw hanging limp
from a goitered neck,
and a tongue too short
to lick caved-in lips
parched and pursed by salt.
When she grips your flipper
in her death-grip
somehow you know
this is all your fault.

A VERSATILE WOOD

I'm no woodsman, but I cut a switch from the poison tree.
I chew and spit the bark of the poison tree –
it cleans my teeth and lowers my blood pressure.
I identify the poison tree from its leaves, its silhouette.
The poison tree bears no catkin, drupe, or fruit.

This writing box is made from the wood of the poison tree.
Not pearwood as I previously thought – poison tree.
One reclusive Japanese designer now works with poison
                                                    tree wood.
This paper is sourced from sustainable poison tree forests.
(Unfortunately it is not acid-free.)

My grandfather and father were woodsmen. I'm mostly angry.
I go around being honest with my friends, my wife –
the anger grows and grows. It grows like anything.
I talk about my anger and my anger listens, delighted,
a poisonous smile on its face.

I come to my senses and find a wood-axe in my hands.
I can make out my handiwork
stacked around me in the dark woodshed:
cord on cord of poison tree logs.
Enough to last winters – as many winters as I can stand.

Now I've got enough poison tree paper for a lifetime of writing,
enough poison tree lumber to build a chapel
with just enough left over to knock together a coffin
and a small sign for the crossroads that reads:
He lies under the poison tree. Be warned.

HAIKAI: SHOEHORN

(Left Foot)

From home to home, it lurked among the umbrellas
to force one thing into another, for want of a Cinderella.

It was the civil
tongue I couldn't keep: cut out,
caned, and set in steel.

Not a proud horn, lost
as the boot descended from
the rhinoceros –

but like cattle-prod
named for its victim – to cram
'sashayed' into 'shod'.

Any shoe can fit
if you take off your sock or
whittle down your foot –

but snug inside each pirouette and victory-march
lurks the curse of the ingrown nail, the fallen arch.

(Right Foot)

Since things that don't fit have to seem to fit,
a shoehorn's a useful heirloom to inherit:

each heel rides its slide
into wingtip or Oxford
or any tanned hide.

Its chromed spoon reflects
every time I tie the knot
why I genuflect:

down in the round hole
square pegs must, when style demands,
breathe out their parole.

For form's sake, we kneel
to preserve the dark expanse
between tongue and heel.

Then standing what we can, and shoeing what we can't accept
we sidestep the spot where our fathers fell in step.

OLD CAMBUSCAN

Once careless, and content with marvellous things –
brass of the brass ring and the clockwork horse,
a daughter who could make a raptor sing,
massed cavalry tactics, Tartar sauce –

I've seen through truth and trickery's divorce,
my banquet table's every dish the same:
horse soup, horse bread, horse mousse, horse coffee-cream –
all saddle-meat, dressed up to seem diverse,

while lasso's ring and magic mirror's frame
equally circumscribe a face long trained
in rope-tricks and the false retreats of fame –

to vanish into myth, and leave behind
quaint fantasies to smooth your suffering –
like bastard swords that heal as well as wound.

ALECTRYOMANCY

The rooster chose the emperor.
Iamblicus set it like a monster

against reason in a scratched circle.
Rough hands stropped horn and wattle,

then yanked the stop-cock of destiny –
flung down the bird to peck the heir of porphyry

from its alphabetical halo.
You might call it the first game show.

Now we watch a sparse rain strut and peck
loose barley from November's burlap sack,

poor grist to sandbag winter's seeping shadow.
Not bags of corn, not bags of silver

can stand as levee for an empire
when shadows like that shadow start to grow.

Those uneasy pagans couldn't have foreseen
all divination's end in scattered grains:

their grand prize was a bigoted Nicene.
This time it will be something quite the same,

or something similar, for both king and cock:
the worried brood peck at their ballot papers

while the feak-faced, distracted soothsayers
smooth ruffled feathers, glance at the chopping block.

MAGPIE

There's accusation in your gaze,
sour superstition on your breath –
in words like 'thief' and 'cannibal' –
but I've bet long and seen my money double
while you were wasting all your thoughts on death.
You fumble through each morning's mysteries
of rings and chains and misplaced keys –

all your accessories that give no access –
while I fasten my diamond tongue-stud
clear as a drop of Satan's blood
and at the twitch of your sprinkler's denials, thrice
gargle and spritz to clear my voice
before my stand-up routine

on the One True Cross.
You accuse me of 'ill deeds' –
look again. These are spats, not widow-weeds.
I was mascot of the bacchanal
when you were doing your worst at school.

You should try giving in to nature:
the gardener knows to tip his hat
and puts up with my sharper's chat,
wise to the difference between bet and better.

Don't look to birds to square your sums,
unearth a coin, a wedding ring, a tiding –
you count for nothing.

While you give me all your traits and qualms,
I take them, and give you nothing in return.

I will remain. I like your lawn.

ODE TO DANAË

Sweet Danny, your daddy bankered you in bronze,
stocked you in a safety deposit box –
a zero-interest hedge against your sons –
collateral in a custom-built Fort Knox
with nothing but a television set
tuned to the 24/7 financial news,
a live link to the Delphic Oracle
droning the red and black in foreign markets –
lean hogs, palm oil, palladium, Brent Crude –
cramming your dreams with futures and short-sells.

But you're the real deal in ten-karat Argos:
a twenty-four karat brain, a guilt-free conscience,
setting your terms for purchase and stop-loss,
doing an MBA by correspondence.
Oh Danny Girl, drowsy in your bronze maze,
love finds its way in on an ion-cloud:
your silk PJ's cling close at its caress –
a charge sparkles the air, glazes your eyes
with gold-film contacts – electroplates a shroud
atoms-thick on your lips, an eerie thinness.

I'm dressed in liquid gold. Your hopes unwrap
the Invisible Man, who's come to set you free –
my disguise drops to fill your two-palmed cup
with Krugerrands and molten rose-gold coulis,
ore smelted with the blood of kings and slaves –
no hush-money but an emancipation,
a salvage-haul from sunken galleons
sleeping too deep to hear the death-loud waves –
wasted gold, brought to light to shine 'em on,
a trust fund for our monster-hunter son.

I know you – you'll assume no debt, no husband –
there's no gilt edge to real security –
you'll assay every nugget in your hand,
heft each gold dollar, doubloon, *fleur-de-lis,*
then give a scrape of each the *aqua fortis.*
Gold is the god that lets you walk through walls,
the golden rigol you can wriggle through –
my Kitty Pride, dolled up in golden fleece –
but you'll weigh every bull run, every obol,
too worldy-wise to think they'll all ring true.

LOVE DOLL RENTAL AGENCY, SHIBUYA

I press the gate buzzer and lower the tone
of the handset hooking me up with the unknown.

The courier drops off an unmarked crate.
I lift her snakeskin body's featherweight

to the light. Her arm drapes over my shoulder
like a rubber boa.

Off the heart-lung pump, she's a plump guilt-spree.
Her lips and seals gleam with petroleum jelly.

Compared to a tattoo's ten thousand punctures
the patches on her punctures seem demure;

two centuries after the patchwork monster's murders,
this is the bride he could have custom-ordered.

Here's someone who will do – and did.
She won't bat an eyelid.

Her voice is motion – the squeak of the Sibyl.
Girls so gorgeous should wear name-labels.

(Actually, her name's on the box,
right above, 'Graduate School of Hard Knocks.')

We spend a quarter of an hour
getting to know each other

over a glass of bubbly in the bath.
She's such an easy person to be with.

But wherever we are, I can somehow hear the sound
of a silent counter counting down.

When we've only got twenty minutes left,
it dawns on me that she's playing hard-to-get:

I twig that she's said nothing for the whole hour,
though somehow I hadn't noticed this before.

A knock at the door. It's the courier.
What weight is this she's slipping out from under?

He offers to help her pack.
I'm a wreck.

We roll her into her bubble-wrap kimono.
My jaw locks in the O of 'Please don't go.'

The courier observes, *You still look bored.*
She answers from the crate, *It's not that hard.*

PROGRESS BAR

You sit there watching it,
aware that something's gone wrong.
This is your life, and your life is no song;
life is no party. We wade through shit,

through toxic garbage up to our knees,
knowing the spigot of an addict's needle
will pierce a callused sole and leave us riddled
as we wade barefoot through the ruined Yangtze.

The world outside has come to pass.
Whether through the bedsit window's safety wire
or the unobstructed view from the fortieth floor,
nothing at all reaches you through the glass.

There might as well be bars
of more than light – black bars across your eyes.
You're soundproofed against everything that dies.
Nature has given up on you – her hollers

grew hoarse when you were still in school –
she floated within reach on that mini-break
ten years ago – vague memories of peaks and lakes –
but you preferred the sound of the pint-pull.

Her corpse snags on the sandbank –
the memory bloats –
something comes back to you about a stolen boat
and a dead man who floated up, or sank.

You can't get up. You hate to sit.
You stare at something being installed –
something lodging itself where the self failed –
and all that you can think to do is stand it.

AN ATOMIC BATTERY IN THE REPUBLIC OF GEORGIA

We knew they'd come to steal our find –
pale men in snow-cats – blank – snow-blind –

reaching with quivering tongs to take
our godlet – their empire's mistake –

as if this rust-set lump of ruby
performed some better ministry

than warming our frostbitten palms –
as if we too kneel before bombs

instead of gods. And here they come –
zipped in lead, whispering *'Strontium.*

Cerenkov.' A two-headed bird
died yesterday, coronas blurred,

and something waits under my skin –

a knot, the sort my axe has known –
and I conclude this godlet's sown

some sign of love, some black oak's twin,
next to one vertebra's winged bone.

QIMMIQ MOUNDS

i.

North of sixty degrees, tethered to a sledge, I'm striding
in slow motion, a marionette determined to rebel,
up through the April dawn – no dogs, no snowmobile –
up to a ring of jagged cairns, night-sprung
around Iqaluit or Pangnirtung.

These ice-bricks are more than lifeless:
not stones, not wind-wrecked *inukshuks* –
this barrow's excavated slate-knives are no knives
but ice-sharp hackles of unskinned fur.
I'm standing in the ring of a massacre.

This is no Neolithic triumph over white bears, white wolves –
no cornucopia of meat and fur. This is a cull.
Each forty-kilo brick's a victim, ice-mortared to his next-of-kin –
each undressed lump, moon-hardened to soapstone
is a dead sled dog with a bullet hole in his skull.

ii.

Take this one. Lake-black eyes lensed in frost,
he stares down dawn-glare without a blink.
His throat's cream countershade's clotted with ice;
ice cements the double coat and the rich mane,
traps his corpse in the cold-cast
of his musculature's smallness.

With a dozen trigger-pulls, the maniple's fan hitch
snapped shut to a limp fist.
Now the king dog's on the bottom of the pile:
hocks of wheel dogs and swing dogs make him a crown of tangles
while across the flatlands of the *taimmani* tussle and growl
somebody's feast of twenty thousand souls.

iii.

Out in Frobisher Bay, the pack ice groans with laughter,
slaps its white thigh with a crack
as conflicting accounts of the slaughter go neck and neck.

But whether the Mounties spined us with rifle-shot,
shot the dogs of our road and larder to leave us landlocked,

torpid as the tins of hash on the town shelves –
or whether, as the Mounties say, we shot them ourselves,

dazzled by our new Lee Enfields and prefab huts –
the *qimmiq* are gone, sled-swish and firn-crunch
drowned out by snowmobile's smoker's cough and oil-stench.

iv.

Time picks history clean as a carcass
scavenged down to its armature.
Past evils flee back to the Mother. The *Aurora borealis*
colours justice and injustice
with the even glow of causality.

Ballasted with blood's obsidian, the king dog on the bottom
seeps down to freeze-dried asservation,
to the perpetuity of his own Paleolithic,
a zoological curiosity
dragging an ash-runnered sledge

while across the empty album of the Arctic's
feast-bowl, and over the white gloss of its Gore-Tex
the racing sleds hiss
hauled by imposters in spanking fur suits:
Siberian Huskies. Eurohounds. Malamutes.

CAMERAMAN
(in memory of Simon Cumbers)

A man feels better with something to hold
in his own defence,
or better yet, something to point
like a magic bone – at enemies, at obsolescence,

at anyone who would disagree –
so better a weapon that can strike a man dead
than this millstone of high technology
with nothing but the power to go on the record.

When they turn their guns on you, you don't have time to beg –
and even if you had the time, you wouldn't –
knowing what's at stake through all the years you've pulled
focus on people ready to kill for belief –

though you've turned the tables on them, since you're the one
closer to what it meant to be a prophet:
steady-handed to the end,
beaming the truth out over wireless

as the murderers close in – keeping the frame tight –
outlived only by the odds, and luckier colleagues
who've limped through deserts, balanced on broken legs,
walked backwards through Afghanistan

with burned hands, or a bullet in the arse,
and kept the camera rolling
through riots – through falling bombs –
white phosphorus –

And so you went – weighed down only in body:
let's say a saint, long-martyred in the practice
of carrying the kit of the modern alchemist,
knowing what weight it takes

to capture light, and cut it without bias,
knowing that medium and message both have mass –
with all it took for them to take your life
strapped to your body in a black bag full of glass.

PINK DOG

He's dying alone
on the streets of Penang.

I'm watching him cling
to his last afternoon.

I'm saying: in this heat today,
he'll die.

With no shade, nowhere to go
he'll pose for photos.

This is the maximum
love he's got left – no one will touch him.

His fur's completely gone.
He wears disease and sunburn.

Shuffling at me for a stroke,
he stops as I back

off. Even the flies
refuse his sores.

He's six years dead,
but I'm not rid

of the pink dog of Penang
and his drawn-out dying.

He stands shivering away
on my Malaccan rug.

We've traded immortality
and some deeper infection:

he won't obey
though I beg

lie down in the shade, boy,
lie down.

TURTLE
(after Hagiwara Sakutarou, *Kame*)

Made of the cedars,
made of the swamp,
the leftover gods,
and the azure-damp,

heavy and jealous as solid
gold in human hands,
heavy as the swamp is deep,
a pure gold turtle sleeps,

weighing more and more on my mind
the more I consider the stakes:
how quietly it bears its gleam,
its lonely, gleaming ache;

how innately it understands
all tendencies to sink,
and pondering them, descends
down to its own dark legends,

sounding me as it sounds
the azure and the lake –
the aeons' alchemy,
and the soon-forgotten ache

of its transmuted body:
the cold ceramic glaze
of its gold kiln-fired shell
(now dimmed to a bronzegreen hull)

and the rubber rawgold wrinkle
of its flesh, its unfired clay,
its centenarian frailty
a chameleon's display:

flesh that can't back a mirror
or serve for a cup, or a lyre,
and so finds common substance
with our own soul-fire:

with the patterned human soul
whose drop into the shadows
sends a light up through the swamp,
the glimmer of an unquenched lamp

as proof against decay –
as some of us might hazard,
and some only conjecture,
and quite a few deny.

STOAT

Where back of the boathouse
the scum-pool's drier
than it's been all century,
he steps with the lightness
of debutante or dancing-master
through his new pantry.

His late-summer-wear's a little shoddy –
but even out in his housecoat
he's nimble and prim.
No parody
of trickster or thief-stoat
sticks to him:

he could be Da Vinci's,
or Hilliard's improbable ermine
by first snowfall.
Till then his civet's the stench
of beheaded crustaceans –
his surplus kills.

He spots me and skips away
to sip from an egg
and leave intact
his species' clichés:
with a gavotte, and a jig,
and a caveat.

CUTTLEFISH

The heart of the sea
jets its salt propulsion
through a fat artery –

an aortic nozzle
valved to the circulation
of no one animal

but the whole sea's hustle,
its submerged kisses,
its streamlined muscle.

Like the sea
its shifting colours
are its constancy.

Its arms reach
for every heart
that enters the sea:

like yours –
nectophore –
freely afloat –

your sepia heart
that sleeplessly
beats for the whole sea,

that beckons the gulls
to hunt for the bleached
blade at its core.

SEDNA

How long have we been lovers, Sedna?
Have I repressed your sea-coal taste?
Were you my fondling nanny, my arctic fox?
I dream of your blubber-quiver, your seal-grey face,
your musk-ox shoulders, your walrus buttocks.
I laugh in my sleep as you yank me from your ice-
hole. I'm fished. Or you lay me beside
your cavernous heat in the dark
where you glitter and slip with seal oil:
I struggle in your hot grip. You bark.
Outside, the wendigo shakes his razor-wire shackles
and scrapes at your igloo with his starved howls –
but I know you'll smother me in motherhood,
papoose me in lard and tar for my own good.

But then I dream of your hair and I'm not so sure.
There've been nightmares. Your black
braided net covers the sea and drags.
Seal – narwhal – polar bear – they've all drowned,
held under by your oilslick, your burble-purr.
The beluga's nosecone shows your nail-rakes.
Your braids are colossal hairsquid –
their inky cuticles rasp like beaks.
You're an old monster, a gasoline jellybag.
Your fingerless palms, your mitten-hands
slather me in bear-fat to blunt the wind's cutlass
as I kneel before you, tying your bootlaces.
I look up into your pup-face, and accept your claim:
Sedna, Sedna – we've been lovers a long time.

WINTER PASTORAL

Sure, the poets have milked it from first frost
to last March melt-run, stern and hoarse:

there's no Arcadia squirreled away in South Weald
and every shepherd has his market price –

but in this sudden freeze, I'll take icicles
on cottage eves – a run of frozen notes –

I'll trade black ironwork for powdered pines,
the cool of London lights for treacherous fields –

the 'Free Gift with Every Purchase'
for a fresh purchase on how I used to feel.

I'll take it as read that country life's as cruel,
that new money and old vie for position

on B-roads where a tractor beats a Jaguar
and stooks of grouse steam rotting in the sun,

where excess marks one's access to the season
and mocks the wiser use of hound and gun.

Still, I'll trade being in the loop for being at a loss,
the *live in the now, mate,* for living remote –

I'll re-learn the pleasure of doubt
and the measure of better gifts:

bread of wild wheat, milk of one cow.
I'll give up the city like a love affair

that's killing both of us – leave it standing there –
the window-shopping, the high-speed lifts,

the teeming pavements chizzing up their shout-outs
in honks and jeers – sea-deep past soundproof panes

where every gift ends in a ninety-nine,
every 'frozen note' is dusted in cocaine.

THE LONG DÉNOUEMENT

Cassio rules in Cyprus now:
with a silver-handled cane he limps
along the tide-break, pondering how
it all went down – the tramps – the pimps –

wine-pottled soldiers on patrol –
knives in the dark – panic alarms –
pride and the unloosed general
dying in one another's arms.

Down in the island's guts, *it* waits –
though bled to danger – racked and flayed –
up through the dungeon's dripping grates
it wakes the fort with manic brays –

a foghorn to the azure bay
though Venice now's a sultan's spoil
and, fathoms deep, Nereidae
swim through the holes in Turkish sails.

Its screams are queer. Morale is low.
And still, for years, the farce drags on:
an unsolved case for Cassio –
'The Moor's Epithalamion' –

no motive as the mystery grows,
no witnesses – just two dead wives
and one knifed rogue. The mystery grows
deep in the prisoner's goggling eyes –

together – soldier, traitor – bound –
old shark, old patsy, an embrace
no final cut, no burial ends:
a two-backed beast, chained face to face.

COELACANTH

Counterweight to all miniaturized elegance
the coelacanth

plays aeons of Sub Hunt and Battleship
through reef gap and volcanic slope

on his checkerboard of lapis scales
while cuttlefish and sniping eels

lampoon his obsolete fashions:
botonée of fronded fins,

oiled skin, hinged skull.
His answer's deeper than this diving bell.

No roe-spawn,
he's pupped in a balloon,

triple-tailed,
inedible in an unastonished world.

Since no one's told him the Devonian's
long done,

he's impregnable to hype:
the discarded but still running prototype.

When he takes your bait
to the world of crippling light,

rising like the Southern Cross
off Comoros,

it's a sacrificial feint.
He'll see what you can't,

before you drop him back into darkness:
the size and disposition of your forces.

He knows your coordinates. And did –
before you set the sea under a grid,

before you floundered, Adam in search of self,
up from the pressures of the coastal shelf.

ELEGY FOR A PORTRAIT PHOTOGRAPHER
(in memory of Corinne Day)

I remember how you lived, those early years –
sleeping on friends' sofas, shooting with their gear,
always saving, never eating enough –
just so that one day, you could smile down
into that black box in your cradled palms:

at the face in a second-hand Hasselblad's
prism, bending light that glowed or bled
left-right reversed onto the ground glass –
the room, the face, meticulous, inverse –
thumbing the focus wheel for more or less;

not at all the way that Nostradamus
would glance into his salver
to throw another future off the cuff,
his methods as obvious as the amateur's:
shoot enough, and you're bound to get lucky.

Even in the maelstrom
of a job for *Harper's* or *GQ*
one shot would do:
there was a weight behind that single click
in your death-still, death-white hands – a calm

so deep each shot was sharp
even in the last light, even at the lowest speeds –
no more in need of a tripod
than Nostradamus, whose 'tripod in bronze'
was a piece of gear

on which so little depended –
but even still,
a weight of water and bronze,
a deep field lens
that bears on me once again

as I search for some occult diary of yours,
from before those last, undocumented days –
in the eyes of the grim-thin models
in your portfolio –
which I'm still poring over,

enoptromancer,
hoping to find some ghost of you reflected:
your shutter-finger in a teapot's flank,
your face in the open half of a film star's wink,
your profile in brushed aluminium or Perspex –

some artefact
there wasn't time to correct.
And on it goes: you hiding in the grain
of art too careful to expose its hand,
while I keep hunting for a flaw

that you'd reject
if you were here,
a flaw that I'd prefer –
so I'm left leafing through your sharp remains,
searching your subjects for a better subject.

THE HAWK AT KAWA-NO-YU

What do I know of the hawk,
though I've looked him in the eye,
where I've seen the gold-flecked
souls of his old prey?

Naked in a hot river
breathing its sulphates
I eye the hawk
and become the hawk-bait.

Two metres above
my boil and blanch
the golden hawk perches
on a bare branch.

In the Castalian spume
of Kawa-no-yu
he and I will divide
the truth from the merely true:

like these falling leaves
of red *momiji*,
the upturned palms
of a lover's plea –

like this maple leaf
with its red work done,
falling through the steam's
white occlusion.

The hawk won't stoop
to my nakedness –
with nothing to regret,
nothing to confess;

he sends no look, no sign –
but a last red leaf
falls between us –
his honed self, and my grief

that even now I'm still
in love with the hawk and the maple,
a love no leaf, no hawk
can return, or even feel –

a truth that leaves me more full
of love for the old lie,
the anthropomorphic lie,
than the truth in the hawk's eye.

TEETH

The young die first. Back to the earth.
Sewer-pipes shine with their phosphates.
Pulped in sleep, we barter their husks for silver.
In old age they'll bear bridges between them.
Some will awake to crowns of gold, some of amalgam,
and vie for succession over the *hors d'oeuvres*.
Some will be burned back down to their roots
when their rottenness touches a nerve.

All feel the press of wisdom
like locked-in hoplites
standing to their pan-pudding – standing stith
against the satrap's minions.

Just like Cadmus, I too wanted a kingdom.
For a set of earth-sprung brothers of Thebes
I sowed my saved-up molars under the elms,
lisped a spell from the broken ranks of my gums –
a gap as wide to my ambitions
as the chink between Pyramus and Thisbe.
I still feel for it with my tongue –
and still no Spartoi come.

HORHOG

On special nights
there's hunter's food:

a marmot (they call it
the 'golden meat')

or thankfully tonight
a goat

stuffed with red-hot rocks –
roasted, then skinned,

jointed, and eaten
with bare hands

and a clasp knife.
I get through a few ribs

doing my stage-makeup
in goat-grease

then spend what feels
like a night and a day

carving the keech
off two vertebrae.

When I drop the stripped
bones on the slab

Ükha shakes his head
and picks them up.

Two minutes later
his blade has scraped

the bones to perfect
desert-white

as if to cost
the sheep-lizards

and goat-beetles
their widow's mite.

And so I learned
how most work goes:

it doesn't matter
how many times

you've turned a morsel
or made a cut

or pushed back from the table
saying it's done:

there's always more meat
left on the bone.

HAIKU: *TSUYU*, NOJIRI-KO

I ran from my selves
to Lake of the Black Princess –
Queen of the She-Wolves.

Blue gas on the ring:
in the last rains of July
my black tea's steeping.

Cabin-builders curse
like Lugh, hammer like Vulcan –
but by five, they're ghosts.

Dusk – some insect plods
carefully up my right shin:
will I look – or not?

Stretched on the boat dock
I read Graves in a light mist,
lost in the *post hoc*.

The pre-season crowd
skirts my towel like a leper's:
alone, therefore odd.

In peripheral
vision, a rainstorm sunset –
the grey light, fool's gold.

On the lake, lightning:
in the flash, each raindrop hangs
a diamond earring.

Lightning through the moon:
the last brush-stroke of '*naka*'
in yellow neon.

Coffee at midnight:
watch that Nojiri hopper
twitch in the lamplight.

He couldn't suspect
in an hour he'll be cocooned
in wolf-spider silk.

This bottled spider's
wound tight – calm in my torch-light
as a prison choir.

It's long past bedtime:
hang the trash from the rafters.
Make the damned mice climb.

A steel door slams tight
on your urban rationale –
thunderclap at night.

The drowned Black Princess
is throttling me in the lake:
I wake with a gasp.

God knows the goddess
deserves more than a cabin –
puts up with much less.

My hardworking muse
has strict standards of living:
write her some new shoes.

A moth on the pane –
feather-duster at dusk, but
by night, Blind Pew's cane.

That elm is no elm,
outlined by lighting: a hunched
night-hag, caught on film.

Every horror film
I've seen turns out to be real
in this sudden calm.

The *o-furo* moans
into life, short-circuited:
a witch's cauldron.

Through the percussion
of its pump I hear the chant
of the lake's coven.

So, 'Night thoughts are best'?
Would he still say that, tangled
up in this mare's nest?

Watching the dawn creep
over the pine wood's wet edge:
at last I can sleep.

Ajisai mopheads
bloomed in the flood: sweet poison
fireworks in lapis.

There must be a leak
in my old rainwater tank –
the drought's ironic.

Now the Black Princess
slumbers on the lake-bottom,
my pen in her fist.

I've swallowed my fill
of rainy season – this frog
can't stay a tadpole.

Notes & Acknowledgements

Many thanks to Paul Rossiter for his insightful and incisive reading as Isobar editor; Jeff Dunmall and Ka-Ping Yee for being my sextant; Leo Critchley and William Demiri-Watson for intense research sessions on everything from medievalism to mathematics; Evelyn, Jeffrey, and Martin Burrett for putting up with a poet; and Estelle, Keith, and Elinor Simons for making one.

❧

TATAMI (畳) 'A rush-covered straw mat which is the usual floor-covering in Japan and the size of which (approx. six feet by three feet) functions as a standard unit in room measurement' (*OED*). New *tatami* give off a scent not unlike fresh-cut grass or hay.

UNI (ウニ・海胆・海栗) The Japanese word for sea urchin. As a foodstuff, *uni* (雲丹) (literally, 'vermilion cloud'), is one of the most celebrated varieties of *sashimi* and *sushi*, and is sometimes enjoyed live directly from the shell. *Nishoku-don* (二色丼): a 'two-coloured' *donburi*, or rice bowl, containing red salmon roe and golden sea urchin roe. *Ika* (イカ): squid or cuttlefish.

THE PRAIRIE BOY REMEMBERS A PAGE IN *DOCTOR NO* See Ian Fleming, *Doctor No* (Jonathan Cape, 1958) (Penguin Books reprint, 2002), 74.

MARCELLUS 'Something is rotten in the state of Denmark' (*Hamlet* 1.4.90). Although Hamlet confides in both Horatio and Marcellus, the latter vanishes from the play after Act 1, Scene 5.

KUROGO In Japanese kabuki theatre, the *kurogo* (黒衣) (literally, 'black clothes') or *kuroko* (黒子) are 'shadows': stagehands and scenery operators, dressed in black and wearing black hoods. In the early days of *kabuki*, they accompanied the performers and illuminated their faces with candles.

AS HE LIKES IT 'Helena' here refers to the heroine of *All's Well that Ends Well*, not the lover of Demetrius in *A Midsummer Night's Dream*.

OLD CAMBUSCAN In Chaucer's 'The Squire's Tale', Cambuscan is a King of Tartary. The tale offers a romance interpretation of the historical Chinggis Khan.

ALECTRYOMANCY Divination by cockerel. A circle is drawn on the ground, with the letters of the alphabet spaced evenly around it. A grain of corn is placed on each letter, and a cockerel set loose in the centre of the circle. The order in which it pecks the grains spells out the prognostication. Iamblichus of Apameia (not to be confused with Iamblichus Chalcidensis in the reign of Constantine) was a Syrian Neoplatonist in the reign of Emperor Julian, and likely died at the end of the reign of Emperor Valens. An apocryphal story suggests that Iamblichus and Libanius used alectryomancy to warn Valens about potential successors, thus inadvertently leading to the rise of Theodosius I. (See for example *Brewer's Dictionary of Phrase and Fable*.)

MAGPIE Scottish lore suggests that the magpie carries a drop of Satan's blood under its tongue. Another legend suggests that the magpie was either the only bird not present at the crucifixion of Christ, or that it was present but did not sing to comfort the dying Jesus, and was therefore cursed.

ODE TO DANAË Danaë was daughter of King Acrisius and Queen Eurydice of Argos. Acrisius imprisoned Danaë after a prophecy indicated that he would be killed by Danaë's son. Zeus came to her in a shower of gold, and she gave birth to Perseus.

See for example Apollodorus, *The Library, Volume 1: Books 1-3.9*, tr. James G. Frazer (Cambridge, MA, 1921), 2.2; Ovid, *Metamorphoses*, tr. Arthur Golding (London, 1567), 6, ll.120–1. The poem follows the form of some of Keats' odes (ten-line stanzas rhyming ABABCDECDE).

AN ATOMIC BATTERY IN THE REPUBLIC OF GEORGIA Engineers in the former Soviet Union frequently used small atomic batteries containing Strontium 90 as power sources in remote radio transmitters and military installations. In December 2001 the IAEA recovered two such batteries from a mountainside near Abkhazia in the former Soviet republic of Georgia. Local villagers had discovered the batteries and tried to use them as a heat source, with disastrous consequences.

QIMMIQ MOUNDS *Qimmiq* is the general Inuit word for 'dog', but here specifically refers to the Canadian Inuit Dog, virtually extinct by the 1970s. Some Inuit accuse the Royal Canadian Mounted Police of shooting thousands of the dogs in order to confine the Inuit to towns, and thus end their nomadic lifestyle. The RCMP dispute this claim, arguing that the Inuit abandoned or shot the dogs as they transitioned from using dogsleds to snowmobiles.

CAMERAMAN Simon Cumbers (1968–2004), Irish-born freelance journalist. Cumbers retrained as a cameraman in the 1990s. He was working for the BBC as Frank Gardner's cameraman when the two men were shot by Al Qaeda sympathisers in Riyadh. Photographers often refer to the lenses they carry as their 'glass.'

SEDNA Sedna, the 'Mother of the Sea', is the Inuit goddess of the sea and marine animals. She also rules Adlivun, the Inuit underworld. The name Sedna has been adopted by a large Canadian oil and mining corporation.

THE LONG DÉNOUEMENT 'LODOVICO [*to Othello*] Your power and your command is taken off | And Cassio rules in Cyprus. For this slave, | If there be any cunning cruelty | That can torment him much and hold him long, | It shall be his' (*Othello* 5.1.331–5).

ELEGY FOR A PORTRAIT PHOTOGRAPHER Corinne Day (1962–2010), British photographer. Although Day used a Hasselblad medium-format camera, she did not do so regularly until 2008.

THE HAWK AT KAWA-NO-YU Kawa-no-yu (川の湯) (literally, 'hot spring river'), is a river hotspring bath in Gunma Prefecture. *Momiji* (紅葉) (literally, 'red leaf') refers to the Japanese maple (*Acer japonicum*).

TEETH   Cadmus created the Σπαρτοί (*Spartoi*, literally 'sown men') by sowing the teeth of the slain serpent or water-dragon that had guarded the Ismenian spring. The surviving Spartoi helped Cadmus build the city of Thebes. See Apollodorus, *The Library, Volume 1: Books* 1–3.9, tr. James G. Frazer (Cambridge, MA, 1921), 3.4.1; Ovid, *Metamorphoses*, tr. Arthur Golding (London, 1567), 3, ll.1–137.

HORHOG Horhog is a roast-meat banquet – rather than the usual boiled stew – served on special occasions in the Mongolian *gobi*.

ۮ

HAIKU: *TSUYU,* NOJIRI-KO *Tsuyu* (梅雨) (literally 'plum rain'), is the Japanese rainy season in June and July. Nojiri-ko (野尻湖) is a glacial lake in the town of Shinano, Nagano Prefecture. The nearby Kurohime Kougen (黒姫高原), the 'Black Princess Highlands', are home to the legend of the Takanashi family whose daughter spurned the advances of a water dragon living in Yagura Pond (岩倉池). In revenge, the dragon created a flood that eradicated the Takanashi line. See the *Nihon densetsu sousho: Shinano no maki* (日本伝説叢書　信濃の巻) (1917), pp.132–4.

'the last brush-stroke of *naka*'. *Naka* (中), the Japanese character for 'centre', 'inside', or 'middle', is written correctly with a final long vertical stroke.

Nojiri hopper. A kind of dark brown *ko-orogi* (コオロギ), or cricket, with long, curling antennae, commonly found around Lake Nojiri.

o-furo. The general Japanese word for 'bath', but also a traditional Japanese bathtub; the modern *o-furo* is often fitted with an electrical recirculating pump.

Ajisai. The blue Japanese hydrangea, *ajisai* (アジサイ) (*Hydrangea serrata*), called mountain hydrangea or 'tea of heaven', blossoms prolifically in the wet acidic soil of Lake Nojiri during rainy season. A kind of naturally sweet tea, *ama-cha* (甘茶) is made from its leaves – although hydrangea leaves in general are somewhat toxic.

www.ingramcontent.com/pod-product-compliance
Lightning Source LLC
Chambersburg PA
CBHW031210090426
42736CB00009B/857